JE 2 0

JE 2 0

HANDMADE by ME

Cement Crafts

Alix Wood

PowerKiDS
press

Published in 2020 by Rosen Publishing
29 East 21st Street, New York, NY 10010

Editor: Eloise Macgregor
Designer: Alix Wood

Projects devised and created by Ben Macgregor

Photo Credits: Cover, 1, 4 bottom, 6, 7, 10, 11, 12, 13, 14, 15, 16, 17, 18, 19, 20, 21, 22, 23, 24, 25, 28, 29 © Ben Macgregor; 3, 4 middle, 8, 9, 26, 27 © Alix Wood; 4 top, 5 © Adobe Stock Images

Cataloging-in-Publication Data

Names: Wood, Alix.
Title: Cement crafts / Alix Wood.
Description: New York : PowerKids Press, 2020. | Series: Handmade by me | Includes glossary and index.
Identifiers: ISBN 9781725302945 (pbk.) | ISBN 9781725302969 (library bound) | ISBN 9781725302952 (6pack)
Subjects: LCSH: Cement--Juvenile literature. | Handicraft--Juvenile literature.
Classification: LCC TT160.W65 2020 | DDC 745.5--dc23

Manufactured in the United States of America

CPSIA Compliance Information: Batch #: CSPK19
For Further Information contact Rosen Publishing, New York, New York at 1-800-237-9932

Contents

Making Gifts from Cement

You might think of cement as just being used for construction, but it is really **versatile**. You can make plenty of cool gifts using ordinary cement.

These decorated eggs were made by filling real eggshells with cement!

It Gets Messy!

Working with cement is messy. You will need to protect your work area with plastic sheeting, and wear old clothes. We recommend mixing your cement outdoors in an old bucket. And always have an adult present while you make your cement crafts, just in case!

You Will Need ...

- cement
- **latex** or **vinyl** gloves
- an old bucket and some water
- plastic sheeting
- a measuring cup
- a trowel
- **acrylic paint** and paintbrush
- everyday household items such as card stock, cooking spray, cardboard, scissors, and tape

What Cement Should I Buy?

A cement mix that already has the sand added makes mixing it much simpler, as you just add water. We used a fence post cement, and did all the projects in this book using around 60 pounds (27 kg) of cement. If your cement doesn't have sand added, you will need to buy some sand as well.

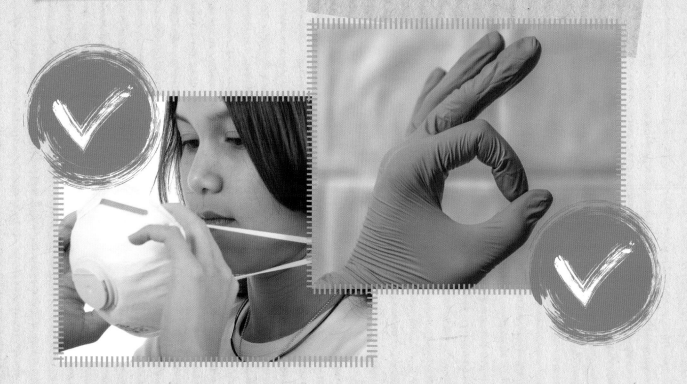

IMPORTANT - Cement powder can irritate your eyes, **lungs**, and skin. Wear goggles, a dust mask, and latex or vinyl gloves when handling cement. Some people are **allergic** to latex, so check if you might be before you wear latex gloves.

Cement Skills

Read up on your cement skills here, such as how to mix perfect cement, get rid of air bubbles, ease set cement out of its **mold**, and keep your cement from cracking.

How to Mix Cement

▲ Put four plastic cups of cement mix into a bucket. If you are using sand and cement instead, mix 3 cups of sand with 1 cup of cement, and mix well.

▲ Gradually stir water into the mix, using a trowel. How much water you need depends on how damp the sand is. Add a little at a time and mix it in.

▲ Keep adding more water until the mix is the **texture** of peanut butter. Make sure the cement is mixed thoroughly.

IMPORTANT -
Don't clean your bucket and trowel in the sink. Cement will clog your drains. Wait until the cement has dried and then flake it off into the trash.

Air Bubbles

When you fill a mold with cement, air bubbles can get trapped inside the mix. The bubbles create holes in the cement. To get rid of air bubbles, either tap your mold on a firm surface or tap the sides of the mold. The air bubbles will rise to the surface.

IMPORTANT -
Don't eat around cement. Cement dust can get on your food and end up inside you.

Filling Molds

Once your cement is mixed, you're ready to fill your mold. Just about any container will work. Spray your mold with cooking spray first. This helps the set cement come out more easily.

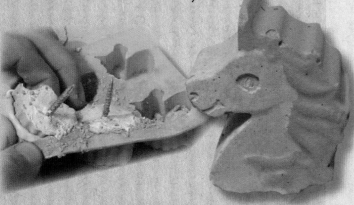

To make these unicorn drawer knobs, we poured cement around a screw placed in a unicorn-shaped silicone ice cube tray.

Drying Tips

In hot, dry weather, cement can crack if it dries too fast. To prevent this, cover your project in plastic wrap or a plastic bag to slow down the drying process.

Make sure your object is COMPLETELY dry before removing it from its mold. It is best to leave it to dry overnight.

Candlesticks

These cement candlesticks are really easy to make and look fantastic. You can use any small container as a mold. A small yogurt container works well.

1 Coat your container with cooking oil spray.

You Will Need ...

- mixed cement
- a trowel
- a small container
- cooking spray oil
- an old candle
- acrylic paint and brush

2 Fill the container with cement mix until nearly at the top, but leave a little space.

3 Push an old candle halfway into the cement. Tap the container on a table to remove any air bubbles. Leave it to dry.

4

Gently pull on the candle to remove the candlestick from the container. Twist the candle to ease it out of the candlestick.

5

Paint your cement candlestick using acrylic paint and a small paintbrush.

MORE IDEAS

Add a little acrylic paint to the water before you mix it into the cement, and you can make a colored candlestick! Don't add much, or it will keep your cement from setting.

TIP - if your candle or candlestick won't budge, run the mold under warm water for a minute.

Stepping Stone

You could make a whole pathway of these beautiful stepping stones! But even one makes an interesting gift for someone to treasure.

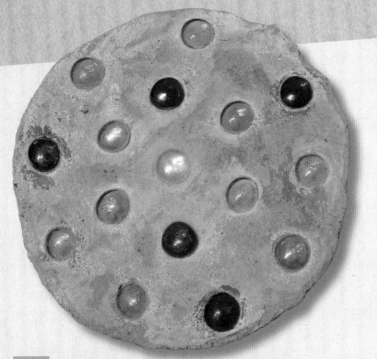

1

▲ Fill your container with cement using a trowel. Tap the container to get rid of any air bubbles.

2

▲ Smooth out the cement using a palette knife or old kitchen knife.

3

▲ Once you have decided on your design, start placing your decorative stones into the cement.

4

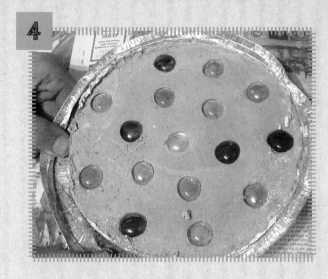

▲ Leave the stepping stone to completely dry, for around 24 hours. Then remove it from your container.

Now you can give your stepping stone to that special someone. It makes a really useful, thoughtful gift.

MORE IDEAS

You can decorate your stepping stone with an **imprint** of your hand. Put on a latex or vinyl glove and press your hand into the cement.

Doorstop

This simple doorstop would look good in any home. The thick rope handle makes it easy to move around. If you don't have any rope, make some by braiding three lengths of scrap fabric.

You Will Need ...

- mixed cement
- a trowel
- cooking spray oil
- a plastic container
- some thick rope
- acrylic paint and brush

▲ Tie a knot to join the two ends of your length of rope.

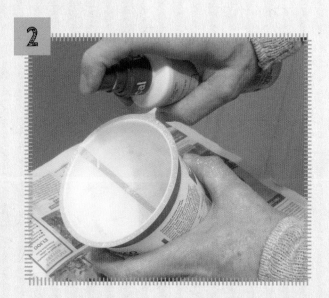

▲ Coat the inside of your container with spray oil.

▲ Fill about a third of the container with mixed cement.

4

▲ Place the knotted end of the rope into the container.

5

▲ Continue filling the container with cement around the rope. Wait about 24 hours for the cement to dry.

6

▲ Snip the edge of the container with scissors and peel the plastic away.

You can paint your doorstop if you like, using acrylic paint.

MORE IDEAS

Your doorstop doesn't have to be round. You could use a small cardboard box as a mold.

Tea Light Pillow

Try making this cool cement pillow. It's great for holding a **tea light**, or using as a bowl to keep trinkets in. It's super easy to make.

1

▲ Place your cement mix into a ziplock bag using a trowel until it is three-quarters full.

You Will Need ...

- mixed cement
- a trowel
- a ziplock bag
- scissors
- a ball, duct tape, and a board
- a tea light candle
- sandpaper
- acrylic paint and a brush

2

▲ Zip the bag shut. Shake the bag to get rid of any air bubbles.

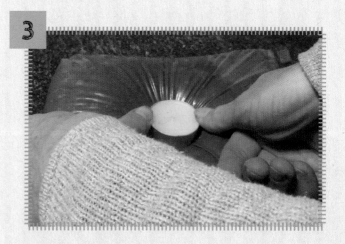

3

▲ Lay the bag on a board. Press a tea light into its center.

4

▲ Place a ball over the tea light and tape it in place around the board. Leave the cement to dry.

5

▲ Once the cement is dry, cut away the bag using scissors. Sand any rough edges using sandpaper.

MORE IDEAS

Your pillow could be used as a plant stand, too. Maybe gift it with a tiny cactus plant instead a tea light.

6

▲ You could paint your pillow with a fun design.

Mini Skate Park

You Will Need ...

- mixed cement
- a trowel
- cooking spray oil
- large foil baking tray
- two small bowls
- acrylic paint and brush

Do you know anyone who loves skateboarding or BMXing? This mini skate park is great for finger skateboards or mini BMX bikes.

1

▲ Position your bowls to create your skate park design.

2

▲ Coat the bowls and the foil dish with spray oil.

3

▲ Fill the foil dish with cement mix using a trowel, until it is three-quarters full.

4

▲ Press the bowls into the cement. Add more cement around the bowls and smooth the surface using the trowel.

5

▲ **Wait at least 24 hours before removing the bowls. Then sand and paint your skate park.** ▼

MORE IDEAS

You could make a box for your skate park. Cut the bottom from a carton and fill it with cement mix. Once dry, remove the cement box and paint it to match your park.

Now your skate park is ready for action!

Solitaire Board

Have you ever played **solitaire**? It is a fun strategy game you can play by yourself. This game board might make a good gift for a grandparent.

1

▲ Place a plate on some cardboard. Draw around it. Cut out the circle. Cut some strips of card stock.

You Will Need ...

- mixed cement
- a trowel
- cardboard and card stock
- 33 marbles
- cooking spray oil
- a plastic bowl
- a palette knife

2

▲ Create your mold by taping the strips around the circle. Alternatively, you could just use a round container.

3

▲ Fill your mold with cement mix. Smooth the surface using a palette knife.

4

▲ Press the plastic bowl into the cement to mark a circle. Then remove it.

5

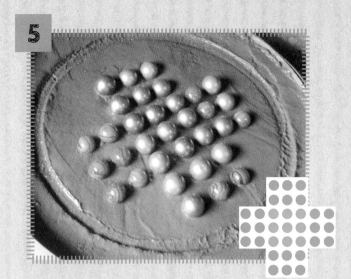

▲ Gently press the 33 marbles a little way into the cement, in the pattern shown. It is easiest to start with the square of nine marbles in the middle first. Then replace the bowl and leave to dry.

6

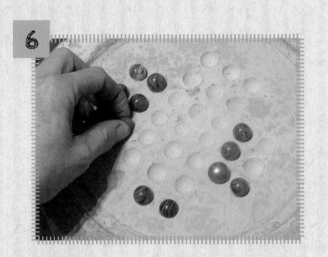

◀ When the cement is dry, remove the bowl. Twist the marbles loose. If some stick, ask an adult to help you.

TIP- spray your marbles with spray oil or they may get stuck!

MORE IDEAS

You can make a really simple tic-tac-toe board. Take a square container and fill it about an inch (2.5 cm) deep with cement mix. Press the game board lines into the cement using a strip of cardboard. Leave to dry. You can make play pieces by painting the letters "X" and "O" on some tiny pebbles.

19

Plant Pot

This **planter** makes a great ornament for a home or yard. Put a small plant or flower in it and give someone you know a special gift.

You Will Need ...

- mixed cement
- a trowel
- small box
- yogurt container
- sandpaper
- small plant

1

▲ Check to make sure your yogurt container fits inside the box, with some room to spare.

2

▲ Put a small layer of cement mix in the bottom of the box. Position the yogurt container, then fill the edges with cement.

3

▲ Once the cement is dry, remove the yogurt container by scrunching it and pulling hard.

4

▲ **Peel away the box.**

5

If the edges are rough,
sand the planter smooth
using sandpaper.

MORE IDEAS

You can make a similar plant
pot using two water bottles
instead. Cut the top off of
a large water bottle. Put in a
layer of cement and then place
a smaller water bottle inside.
Fill the gap and leave it to set.

Put a little damp soil
and a plant in your
plant pot. Pop the
planter in a gift bag
and it is ready to give.

Cement Hand

This cool cement hand is surprisingly easy to make. It could be a soap dish, or maybe used to display an ornament.

1

▲ For this project, you need a latex or vinyl glove.

You Will Need ...

- mixed cement
- a trowel
- plastic cups
- a latex or vinyl glove
- an adult to help you

2

▲ Cut off the bottom of a plastic cup. Push the glove into the cup. Fold the glove's wrist over the top, to help hold it open while you fill it with cement mix.

3

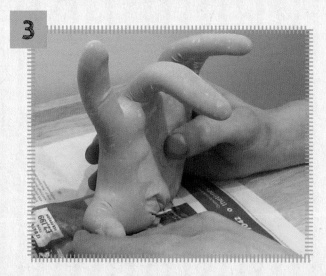

▲ Tie the wrist of the glove in a knot. You may need an adult to help you. Quickly mold the fingers into the shape you want them to be.

4

▲ Tap the glove to get rid of any air bubbles. Use plastic cups or other objects to prop the hand in the correct position while the cement dries.

5

▲ Peel off the glove once the hand has dried.

6

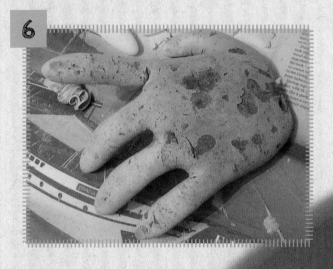

◀ If any fingers break, you can glue them back on. Ask an adult to help you.

Turn it over, and your hand could be a bookend!

Little Table

This amazing little table looks like a magical floating tablecloth! If you turn it upside down it would make a great planter for someone's yard, too. Make sure you ask permission before you use the towel.

You Will Need ...

- a bucket of cement mix
- an old towel
- thick cardboard
- a plastic bag
- scissors
- some strong tape
- a large bowl of water

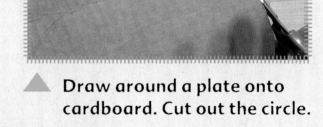

1

▲ Draw around a plate onto cardboard. Cut out the circle.

2

▲ Make a triangular base by folding a rectangle of thick cardboard.

3

◀ Tape the base to the circular top. Adjust the height of the triangle base so the towel will drape onto the floor.

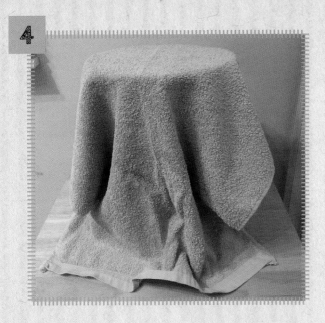

▲ Drape the towel over the table to check the height.

▲ Wet the towel all over with water and then move it around in a bucket of cement mix until completely covered.

▲ Cover the cardboard table with a plastic bag. Drape the towel over the table. Adjust the folds until you are happy, and leave to dry.

When completely dry, take away the cardboard triangle base. The table will stand by itself! →

25

Cement Eggs

A perfect Eastertime gift, these pretty ornamental eggs look great in a bowl on the table. You could hide them around the house to create a fun Easter egg hunt, too.

1

▲ Poke a hole in an egg using a skewer. You can store and use the egg later. Wash the shell.

You Will Need ...

- cement mix
- a spoon
- real eggs or plastic eggs
- a skewer
- an egg carton
- acrylic paint and brush

2

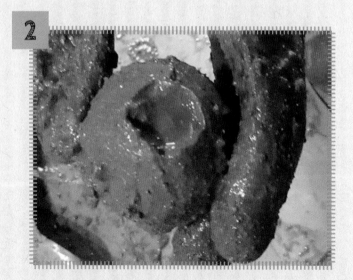

▲ Carefully spoon the cement mix into the eggshell. Put the eggs in an egg carton to dry.

3

▲ Once the cement egg is dry, peel off the shell.

26

MORE IDEAS

You can make cement eggs using plastic eggs, too. Most plastic eggs unscrew in the middle. Open them up and fill each half with cement mix. Press the two halves together and leave them to dry in an egg carton. Once dry, you should be able to twist the eggs and open them. If this doesn't work, soak them for a few moments in warm water and try again.

You can decorate your eggs with paint, or maybe glue some string around the center to hide any marks.

Drink Coasters

Everyone could use these great **coasters** in their life. Make a few and wrap them together to make a useful gift.

1

▲ To make the bases for your molds, trace around a circular object onto card stock.

You Will Need ...

- cement mix
- pen or pencil
- card stock and scissors
- thick cardboard
- tape
- acrylic paint and brush
- palette knife

2

▲ Cut out the circles, and then cut some strips of card stock to make the sides.

3

▲ Tape the sides to the circles, and your molds are ready.

4

To make your patterns, cut shapes out of thick cardboard and glue them in place in the molds.

5

Fill your molds with cement mix.

6

Smooth the surface using a palette knife. Once the cement has set, peel away the cardboard.

Once the coasters have set, paint the shapes, or around the shapes, using acrylic paint.

Glossary

acrylic paint Fast-drying paint that is water-soluble, but becomes water-resistant when dry.

allergic Having an abnormal reaction— such as sneezing, itching, or rashes—to substances, situations, or physical states.

coasters Shallow containers, plates, or mats that protect a surface.

imprint A mark made by applying pressure.

latex Made from a mixture of water and fine particles of rubber or plastic.

lungs The organs forming the special breathing structure of vertebrates that breathe air.

mold The frame on, around, or in which something is constructed or shaped.

planter A container in which ornamental plants are grown.

solitaire A game played by one person.

tea light A small, squat candle in a metal case.

texture The structure, feel, and appearance of something.

versatile Able to do many different things.

vinyl Made from a polymer of a vinyl compound.

Further Information

Books

Kington, Emily. *Monster Mâché Art.* Minneapolis, MN: Hungry Tomato, 2019.

Kollmar, Gail. *Krazy Kool Kinetic Sand!: Play, Build, Stamp, and Sculpt with the Superhero of Sand.* East Petersburg, PA: Design Originals, 2016.

Stephens, Cassie. *Clay Lab for Kids: 52 Projects to Make, Model, and Mold with Air-Dry, Polymer, and Homemade Clay.* Beverly, MA: Quarry Books, 2017.

Websites

Due to the changing nature of Internet links, PowerKids Press has developed an online list of websites related to the subject of this book. This site is updated regularly. Please use this link to access the list:

www.powerkidslinks.com/hbm/cement

Index